"A picture is worth a thousand words"

This purpose of this manual is to help those who teach swimming, especially those with little or no experience, to introduce their pupils to swimming strokes and basic skills.

Good practices are illustrated by sequences of diagrams, showing the required body positions. These guide the teacher using a step by step approach, leading to proficiency.

Many of the sequences use exaggerated teaching points, these are an effective way to get the desired behaviour.

You may see practices other than those shown being used successfully. However, we have selected those which are simple, effective and proven.

CONTENTS

Accidents often occur due to poor organisation. It is therefore the duty of every teacher to prepare thoroughly and think ahead. **Insist** on discipline.

A teacher must be in full control and be able to clear the water within seconds in an emergency.

Check pupils **ability** in shallow water first.

- Skills learnt earlier may be 'rusty'.
- They may not know what is safe in deep water.
- A distance badge does not mean 'deep water safety'.
- A costume covered with badges may be borrowed.

Practices should be just achievable. Avoid injuries by putting your pupils into ability groups.

Goggles should only be allowed when chemicals are a problem, or for medical reasons. As swimming teachers it is our job to teach pupils to use their eyes; after all they would not be wearing goggles if they fell into a river or a canal!

Jewellery should be removed.

First Aid Know where the first-aid kit is kept. Do you have a first-aid qualification? Are you up-to-date?

Telephone A telephone should be accessible. However it may be coin operated. Do you have the correct change?

Depths of the pool should be pointed out to the pupils. Head first entries of any kind must be into a depth of at least 1.8 m, or at least full reach depth of the pupils, which ever is the greater.

Equipment must be put away when not in use. Loose floats can be very dangerous and must be stored. Pupils should do this!

Horseplay in the changing rooms or on the poolside is particularly dangerous due to the wet floors. Pupils should always **walk** and keep well away from the edge of the pool.

School Travel Know your insurance. Travel with a completed register, making a head count before you leave school, and before you leave the pool premises.

Read this before you start!

Between the ages of six and twelve is generally considered to be the prime age for learning a skill. Priority should be given to the basics which will prepare the pupil to acquire the skill.

i.e.
- Safe entries-Safe exits.
- Fun through the use of games and music.
- Floatation and submerging practices.
- Independent travel, using buoyancy aids.

Children learn through imitation.

Ideally, there should be provision for a good demonstration; "A Picture Is Worth A Thousand Words".

- Ensure it is correct. Keep it **simple**.

A skill should be 'Built-Up' in definite stages.

- 'Have a Go' at the whole skill.
- Choose an appropriate practice to suit the ability.
- Build on that practice using successive progressions
- Develop the skill over **short** distances, thus avoiding fatigue and bad habits.
- Practices should be repeated until the movements become natural.

PROGRESSIVE PRACTICES

PROGRESSIVE CHANGE

PERMANENCE

SUCCESS

Teach children to 'feel' through the water.
- Imaginative teaching points.
- Appropriate teaching practices

Children need feed back about their performance. It should be simple, correct and positive and can be verbal or mime (e.g. thumbs up) or reward.

As pupils with disabilities are commonly taught with the mainstream, you should consider taking a course such as the *ASA TEACHER CERTIFICATE (Swimming for people with disabilities).*

Try to get medical certificates and written parental consent before they start their lessons.

Here are some points to bear in mind:

- Your main aim is to develop independence.
- Emphasise the abilities of these pupils rather than disabilities.
- Ensure you have a positive but relaxed attitude. This will give the pupils a motivating and rewarding session.
- Expect pupils with disabilities to put in as much effort as the mainstream.
- Demand high standards, but remember that discarding a chair or other aid and entrusting support to the water is itself a great achievement.
- Be prepared to adapt lessons to the pupils' needs.
- Develop safety skills early. Remember these pupils may be at the learning stage longer than average.
- Use buoyancy aids to promote confidence.
- Learn to recognise the symptoms of common 'invisible" disabilities, and spread this knowledge to the other teaching and pool staff.

PUPILS WITH A DISABILITY

Some 'invisible' disabilities you may come across include:

ASTHMA ... the narrowing of the airways, causing breathlessness and wheezing. About 4 children in 100 suffer from it. It can often be controlled by medication, for example:

Intal - which can prevent an attack if taken half an hour before swimming

Ventolin and **Bricanyl** - which can control an attack in progress.

To help these pupils:

- Vary the strokes, and hence the respiratory demands.
- Ensure pulse and breathing are allowed to recover before the next activity.
- Regular swimming helps increase lung capacity.

EPILEPSY ... attacks caused by sudden abnormal discharge of the brain cells. Many sports are not appropriate for those with epilepsy, but swimming can be helpful. Some pupils will hide their epilepsy, but it is important that you are aware of it. Try to develop an open and trusting relationship.

In an attack:

- Keep calm.
- Support the head.
- Let the fit run its course.
- Don't put anything between the teeth.
- When the fit is over, ensure the pupil lies quietly until consciousness returns.
- Make someone stay with the pupil.

HAEMOPHILIA ... Roughness or firm handling can cause bruising, bleeding, swelling or stiffness. Ensure good organisation and a controlled environment.

BRITTLE BONES ... Pupils tend to be small, with limbs deformed by frequent fractures. Observe them closely during pool side entry and exit. Avoid contact during group work. Deafness is often associated.

CYSTIC FIBROSIS .... affects the digestive system and lungs, which may be infected and blocked with mucus. Have a good supply of tissues - encourage frequent coughing to clear the airways.

HEARING IMPAIRMENT ... Keep close to the pupil, with eye to eye contact. Use body language and mime to reinforce the message. Avoid distractions.

VISUAL IMPAIRMENT ... Again, keep close to the pupil. Give clear, simple instructions. Check frequently that the message has been received. An understanding partner will help.

Entry

The start to your lesson is vital. It should be very positive ensuring that your pupils enter on a given signal. E.g. "You are going to jump onto the black line and.........," Followed immediately by an introductory activity.

Introductory Activity

This sets the tone, is an 'aperitif' before the main theme and therefore should be short and place very little emphasis on technique. E.g. "Swim four widths of your favourite stroke" or "Who is the first person to swim to the other side, climb out and touch the wall?" etc.

Main Theme

(Usually about half your lesson time). Choose the stroke you wish to teach. Teach it for at least three lessons, preferably more. Remember, you have to introduce it, correct it and develop it:

- Let them have a go at the whole skill (assuming they are capable of having a go). Assess their ability and group if necessary, keeping the weak pupils together.
- Decide on the first practice. It is normal to start with a 'legs only' practice, no matter how good the pupils are, in order to improve balance and body position.
- Progress through the practices until you feel your pupils have reached their limit. There is nothing to be gained by progressing further, since they will only develop faults.
- Finally, let them have another attempt at the complete skill and look for improvement. Choose the best performer and allow them to demonstrate to the rest of the group. Ideally the group should then be given the opportunity to copy the demonstrator (if the demonstration was good enough!).

Concluding Activity

(Usually a quarter of the lesson time)

Choose a skill and develop it. E.g. Mushroom float, handstands, surface dives, diving etc. This adds variety and they should leave your lesson with a smile and a desire to return for more.

Teaching Points

Ideally, only **one** point should be given each time you set your pupils off. It should be the **last** thing the hear.

Notes

Safe Entries

Backwards down the steps, for the very nervous pupil.

A swivel entry for the apprehensive pupil.

Jump, aiming for **distance**, for the confident pupil.

Artificial Aids

These are of particular value to pupils with a disability.

Arm-Bands - preferably without inflation, under the arm-pits enabling arms to stay close to the body.

Advantages - safe, more active lesson. Able to co-ordinate arm and leg movements. Independence.

Disadvantage - pupils may come to rely on them if the teacher does not insist that they come off for some part of each lesson.

Swim Belt - gives extra buoyancy; particularly useful to pupils who cannot lift their feet off the pool floor.

Teach your pupils to **use** their floats. Practise all three positions without a pause, moving through the sitting position each time.

Lying on the front.

"Head forward, chin in the water and stretch"

Sitting in the water.

"Press down on your floats"
"Imagine you are sitting in an arm-chair"

Lying on the back.

"Head back, ears under and stretch"

GAMES WITH A PURPOSE....N.B. Arm bands **off!**

Command	**Aim**
Jump high and touch the roof	*Spring & Stretch*
Jump high and spin like a helicopter	*Spring and Rotate*
Jump high then **kneel** on the floor	*Height & Submerge*
Jump high then **sit** on the floor	*Height & Submerge*
Jump high and touch the floor with one **elbow** (or both)	*Rotate*
Jump high and touch the floor with your **chin**	*Rotate*
Jump high and touch the floor with your **ear**	*Rotate*
Float thin like a pin Float wide like a star Float round like a ball Sink like a stone	*Experiment with Floatation*
Spin round like a ball	*Float & Rotate*
Kick like a frog Feet like a penguin Kick as if a motor boat	*Propulsion*

INTRODUCING PUPILS ONTO THEIR BACKS

PRACTICE		TEACHING POINTS
Regaining standing position.	"Head back - lie back" "Stretch and imagine you are lying in bed" "Ears under the water"	"Head up - sit up" "Who can sit up the quickest?"
Legs only. Two floats.		"Tummy up" "Long legs, under the water"
Legs only. Float on chest.		"Chin up to the ceiling" "Knees under"
Legs only. Float extended.		"Stretch from head to toe' "Knees under the float"
Legs only. Arms at sides. Palms touching the legs.		"Silent kick" "Arms straight and palms touching your legs"

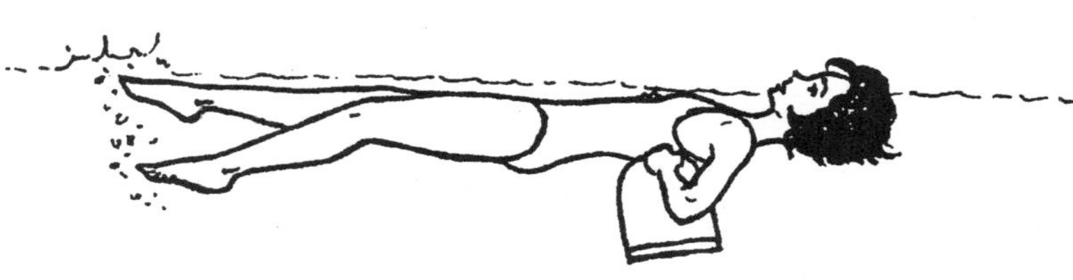

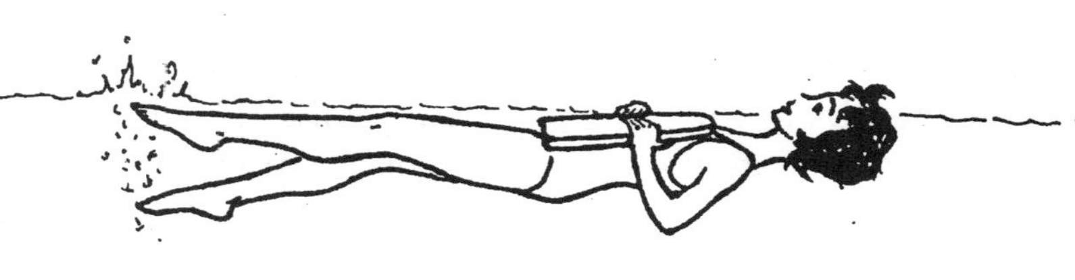

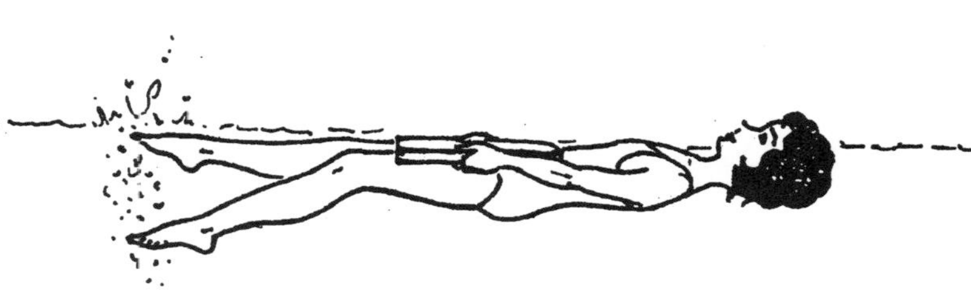

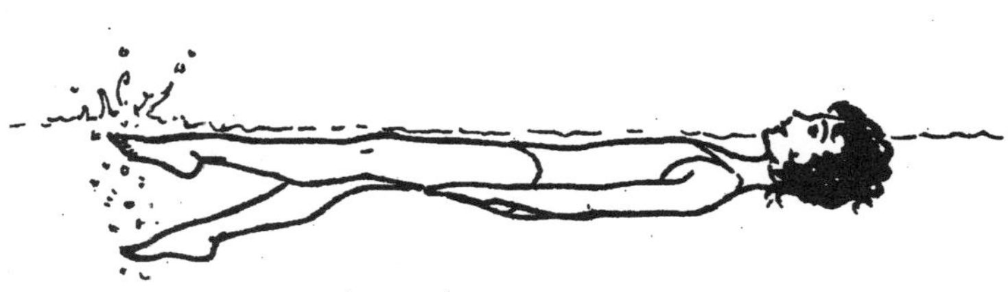

Remember: The head is the **'steering wheel'**

If you want pupils to lie on their backs then the head should be back in the water. If it is not, the body will not travel backwards, but buckle in the middle and eventually sink.

The knees must remain under the water to avoid the head being submerged and to establish an efficient leg action. Hence, **"a silent kick"**.

Pupils should be encouraged to stretch the body throughout. Particularly encourage a straight arm position with the arms close to the sides when working on legs only. The purpose of this is to decrease resistance and to improve floatation. After all, when your pupils are introduced to the arm action, they **do not scull** at the hips at the end of each push phase!

There are two types of arm action. The straight pull is often easier for the beginner. The bent arm pull is more powerful and used mainly by competitive swimmers. If your beginner shows a natural tendency to pull with a bent arm then it should be developed. (Very often, though, they are 'slipping' the water due to weakness in the arm action).

Once you have co-ordinated the arm and leg action to a reasonable standard, encourage your pupils to 'reach' for the entry by asking for a slight roll of the shoulders. This will not only help continuity, but will also prepare them for the bent arm pull.

PRACTICE | **TEACHING POINTS**

Legs only.
Arms straight at sides.
Palms touching the legs.

"Stretch"

"Knees under the water at all times"

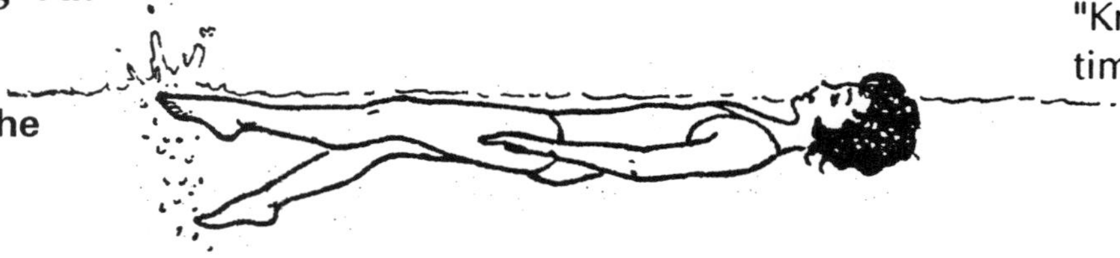

At the rail or standing (Briefly).

"Brush your ear with your arm

"Hand enters little finger first on its side"

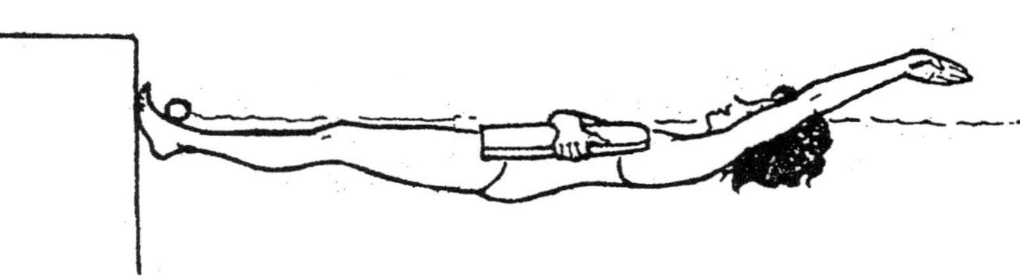

"Push **round** to your leg"

Single arm pulling.

"Straight arm over the water"

"Little finger in first"

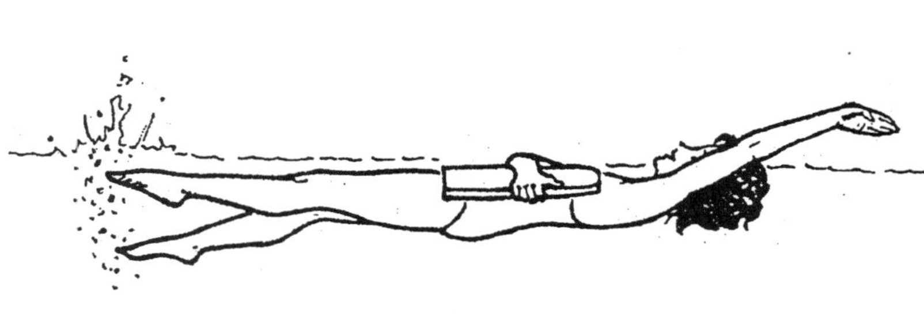

"Silent hands - no splash"

"Shallow push **round** to your leg"

Full stroke.

Stroke your ear...stroke your leg"

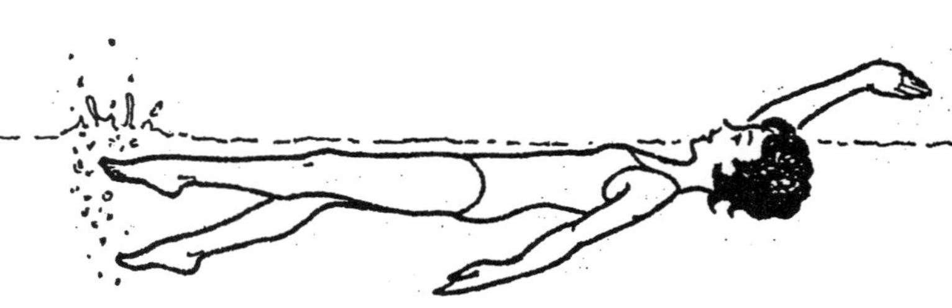

"Reach back for the water...push it to your leg"

Notes

PRACTICE | **TEACHING POINTS**

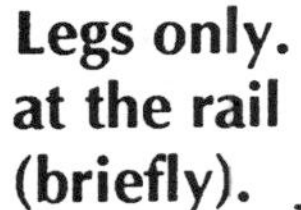

**Legs only.
at the rail
(briefly).**

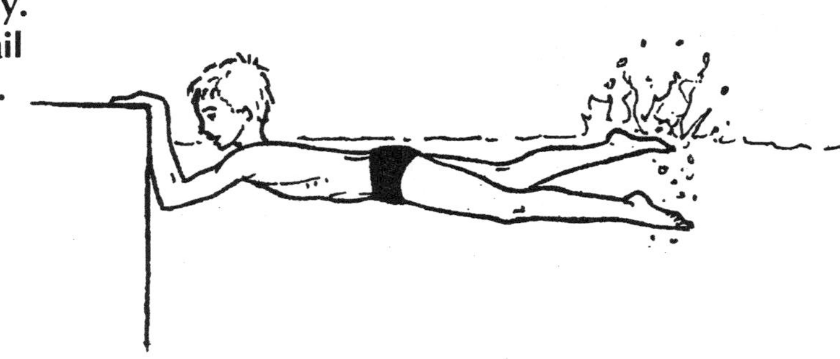

"Keep your heels under the water"

"Long legs"

Legs only.

Two floats.

(Chin low).

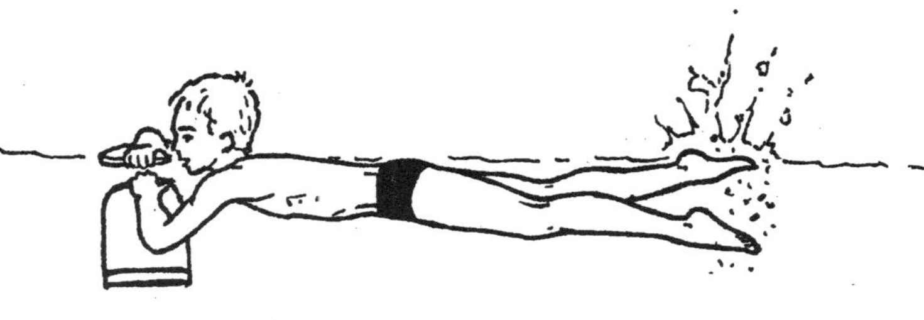

"Pointed toes"

"Loose, floppy ankles"

"Keep your legs close together"

Legs only.

Float extended.

(Encourage head down).

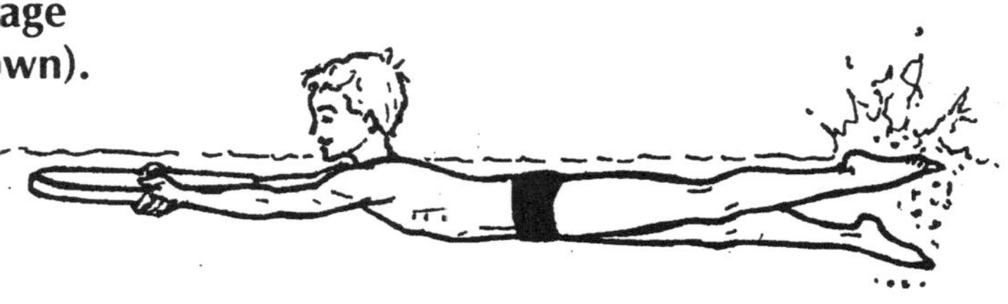

"Swing from your hips"

"Tiny splash"

"Kick hard"

Front paddle

"Keep your hands under the water"

"Tuck your elbows well into your sides"

"Reach forward and push back"

"Imagine your hands are spears. How long can you make them?"

Without doubt, one of the most difficult aspects of teaching swimming is Front Crawl breathing. Many mistakes are made as a result of attempting to teach breathing before the pupil is ready for it.

The basics must be taught very thoroughly and until a pupil can perform the practice 'Full Stroke, no Breathing' there is little point in introducing breathing practices.

Pupils need to have participated previously in many under water activities, to assist them with aquatic breathing techniques.

In a nut-shell, the pupil should only see two areas when being introduced to breathing: the bottom of the pool as they blow **out**, and their shoulder as they suck air **in**. It is often difficult to get them to keep their chins down. The exaggerated teaching point "Touch your **chest** with your chin - Touch your **shoulder** with your chin" can often prove effective as can "Keep one eye in the water."

Pupils should be able to breathe **every** stroke for a distance of about twenty five metres, without encountering any problems, before you can be satisfied they can breathe properly. Beware the pupil who goes through the motions but **holds** their breath!

Repeat practices until they become habitual.

PRACTICE | **TEACHING POINTS**

Legs only.
Float extended (face in the water).

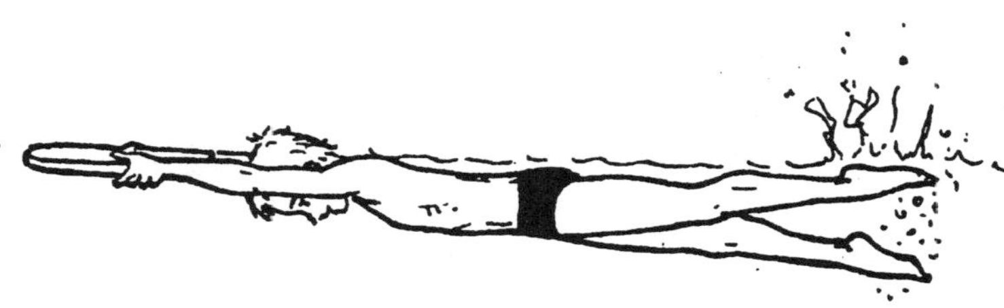

"Arms squash ears"

"Eyes down...eyes open"

"Tiny splash"

Legs only.
Thumbs linked.

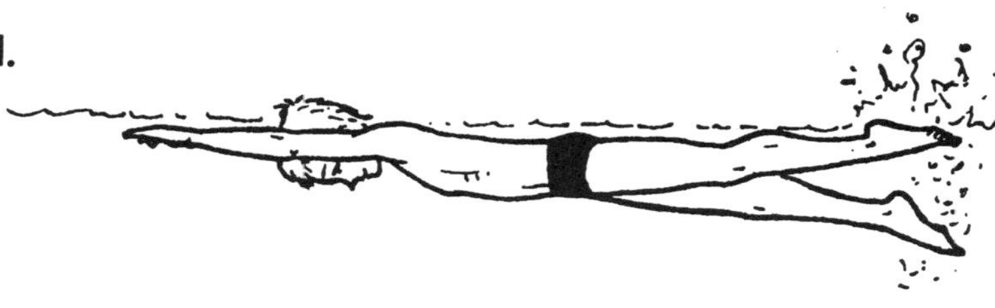

"Legs close together"

"Loose, floppy ankles"

Full stroke.
No breathing (Emphasise arms).

"Finger-tips enter the water silently - no splash"

"High elbow - spear the water like a javelin"

"Push the water back to your feet"

Getting ready for breathing practices

Kick on the side

Head resting on the extended lower arm

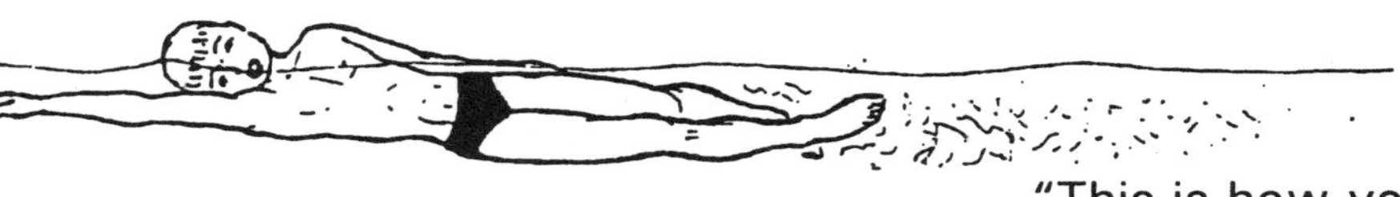

"This is how you will feel when you roll to breathe"

PRACTICE | **TEACHING POINTS**

At the rail.
Exhaling.

Breathing arm holds the rail.

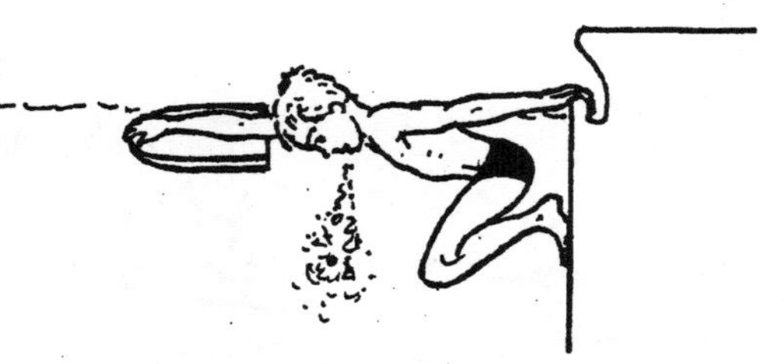

"Both eyes in the water"

"Chin close to your chest"

"How hard can you blow out to the bottom of the pool"

At the rail.
Inhaling.

"Turn your head on its side"

"Keep one eye in the water"

"When your mouth is clear breathe in"

Legs only.
With breathing.

(Remember kicking on the side?)

"Keep your breathing arm 'glued' to your leg."

"Blow to the bottom of the pool, then turn your head and breathe in"

"Blow and roll"

Now add the breathing arm.
Single arm pulling.

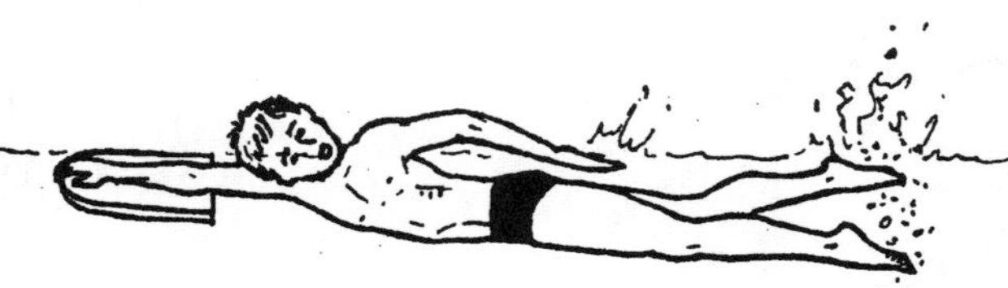

"Remember, think only of your breathing arm – pull and roll"

"Turn your head as you blow your hand towards your leg."

"As soon as your mouth is clear - breathe **in**"

Full stroke.
Breathing every stroke.

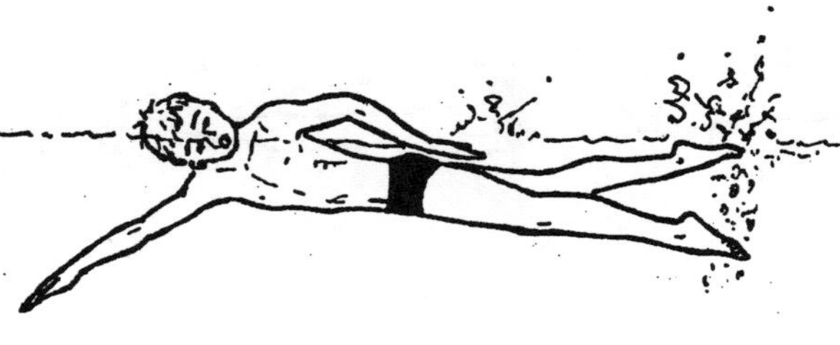

"Are you still keeping one eye in the water"

"Reach for the water, then push it back until your thumb strokes your leg"

Breaststroke is one of the more demanding strokes to teach. Only patience, good observation by the teacher and constant repetition of practices will prove to be effective.

In the early stages of teaching this stroke, it is necessary to encourage a steady head position with the chin remaining in the water throughout. This enables the pupil to breathe without having to move the head. A pupil learning the stroke will only bring the feet out of the water if invited to 'lower' and 'raise' the head throughout the stroke; this will develop quite naturally as the pupil develops power and speed.

It is important to use 'transfer of skill' (as in all practices). For example, if your pupils have just been **sitting** on the pool-side **watching their heels** making circles, then the next practice should be in the water, on their **backs (semi sitting)** with two floats for maximum support, **watching their heels** make circles in the water.

Similarly, after practising at the rail on their fronts they should then practice on their fronts, with two floats for maximum support. This way pupils can put into motion the feeling they experienced when performing static practices.

This stroke in particular lends itself to 'exaggerated teaching points', which can be seen to the right of the diagrams.

There are two types of arm action, both producing continuous circling movements with a short glide. In both cases the movements stay in front of the shoulders.

The straight arm pull is followed by a bend and drop of the elbows. This pull is usually performed with the wider 'recreational' leg action.

The bent arm pull is usually performed with the elbows remaining high as the lower arms and hands drop down and pull backwards. This pull is usually performed with a narrow kick and is used by competitive swimmers.

PRACTICE	TEACHING POINTS

On the side of the pool (briefly).

"Curl your toes up towards your knees"

"Keep your toes up and draw circles with your heels"

"Bend-out-together"

On the back.

Two floats.

"Are your big toes still curled up?"

"Feel your heels push the water away from you"

At the rail.

Elbows pressed against the wall.

"Heels up to your seat"

"Heels touching...turn your feet out like a penguin"

"Are your ankles stiff? Now kick back with your heels"

Two floats.

Knuckles touching.

(Chin in water).

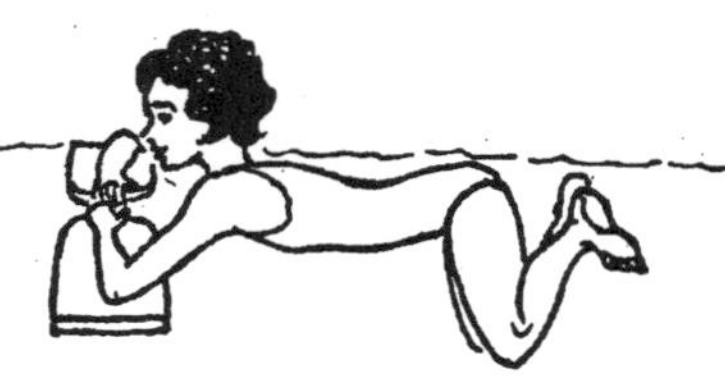

"Have you still got penguin feet?"

"Bend-out-together"

PRACTICE | **TEACHING POINTS**

Legs only.

Float extended.

"Keep your knees close"

"Whip your heels back and stretch"

"Kick in circles"

Inverted breaststroke.

Hands holding waist.

"Heels down and swirl round and together"

"Snap your ankles together"

Full stroke.

Emphasise arms.

"Keep your hands in front of your shoulders"

"Press and swirl - elbows tucked in"

"Reach forward"
"Pull in circles"

DEVELOPING POWER

Legs only.

Count kicks.

(Reducing).

"Bend and whip back hard"

"Snap your ankles together - glide"

Full stroke.

Count kicks.

(Reducing).

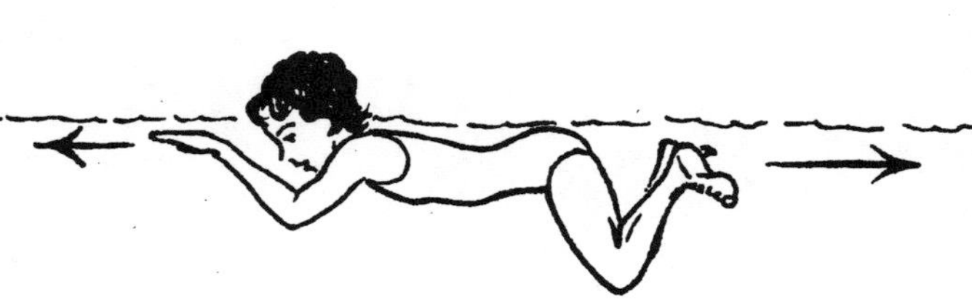

"Blow your hands away from you and stretch"

"Pull, kick and glide"

Notes

Remember! The head is the **'steering wheel'**, particularly in this stroke.

Experience shows that on the whole pupils should be encouraged to "have a go at it" rather than strive to be accurate. Those who achieve any success seem to have natural abilities - flexibility and strength in particular.

It is essential to get good undulation first.

There are three main elements to undulation:

- The head position.
- The bend of the hips.
- An efficient leg action.

The arm action comprises:

- A thumb first entry.
- A Breaststroke sweep out and in.
- A Front Crawl push back to the thighs.
- And a 'flinging' sideways recovery clear of the water.

PRACTICE		TEACHING POINTS
Leg action. **At the rail.**	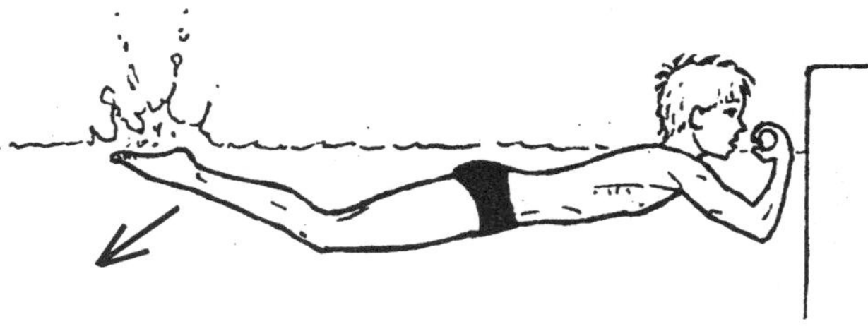	"Glue your legs together" "Keep your heels under the water" "Move from your hips"
Legs only. **Arms at sides.**	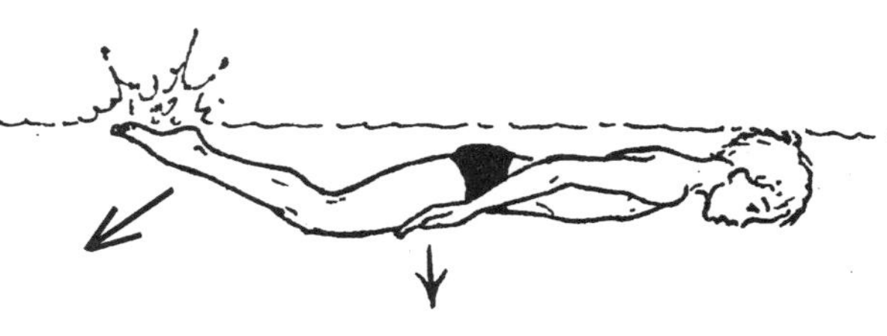	"Move from your head to your toes like a snake" "Kick the water backwards to the bottom of the pool"
Legs only on the back. **Arms at sides.**	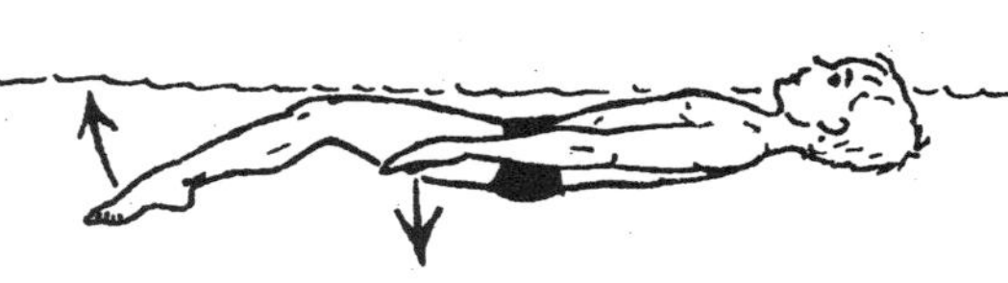	"Kick the water away from you" "Move through your shoulders"
Legs only. **Thumbs linked.**	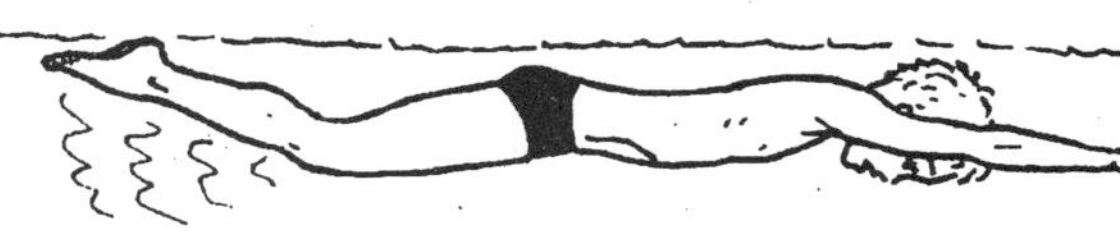	"Keep your head between your arms" "Wiggle from finger-tips to toes" "Kick your hips up to the surface"
Legs only. **Along the bottom.**	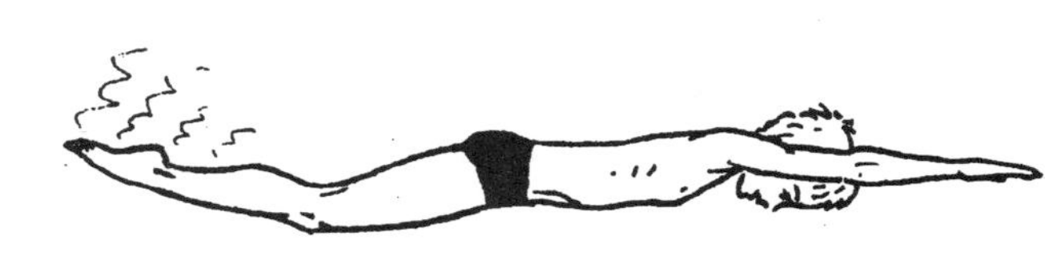	"Loose ankles. Whip the water backwards to the bottom of the pool" "Ripple through the water"

PRACTICE | **TEACHING POINTS**

Single arm pulling

One arm extended
Breathing to the side

"Feel your hand enter in front of your head"
"Glue your legs together"
"Pull and roll"

"Feel your hips close to the surface"

Pattern swimming

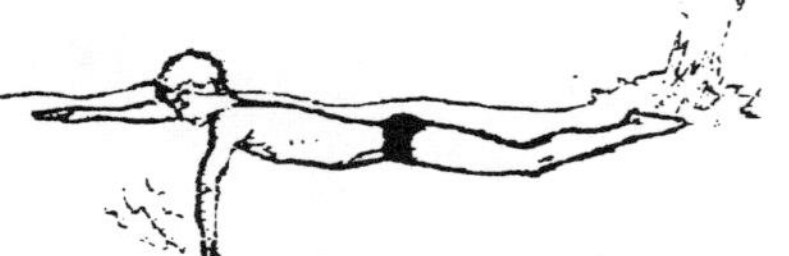
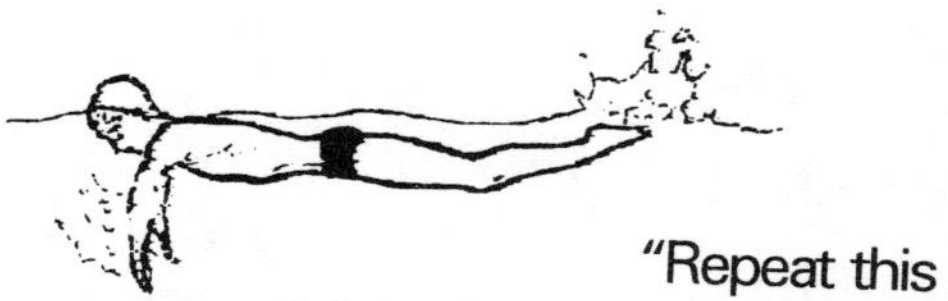

Two right pulls

Two left pulls

One full stroke

"Repeat this sequence as many times as you can"

Full stroke

Breathing every second stroke

"Blow your hands out of the water"

"Kick your hands into the water ... kick hands out of the water"

- **Pupils' final skills are greatly influenced by what they were taught as beginners.**

  Play should have a purpose!

- **Each skill should lead to the next, with a progressive development.**

  An example is 'Pre-requisites to Diving'.

- **Each lesson should finish with the development of under water skills through play.**

SAFETY! SAFETY! SAFETY!

Great care must be taken when transferring pupils to water which puts them out of their depth.

Always have a safety-pole to hand.

Position your pupils so that they face the end of the pool i.e. with a shoulder to the wall. This way, if they move away from the vertical position and start travelling, they will remain close to the wall and within reach.

Wide, slow, giant movements are the secret to treading water. Pupils must create as much resistance as they can to avoid sinking. After all, if we wanted them to sink we would ask them to 'stretch and streamline'. So the opposite is necessary to stay up.

Variations in the leg action can be Breaststroke, Front Crawl or alternating type Breaststroke (often used by Water Polo players and known as an 'egg beater' kick).

NB. Experiment with leg and arm actions whilst in shoulder depth water.

With two floats.

Shoulder to the wall.

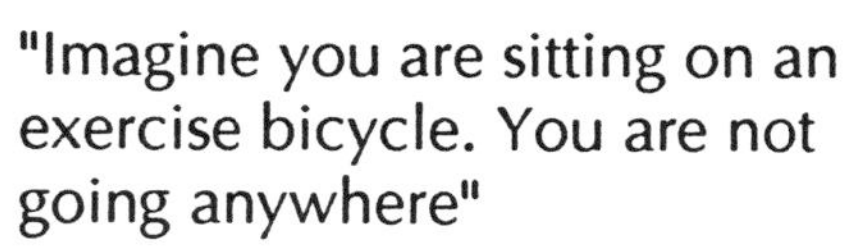

"Imagine you are sitting on an exercise bicycle. You are not going anywhere"

"Look at the end of the pool"

"Wide giant strides backwards and forwards or sideways"

"Choose the leg action you find most comfortable"

With one float.

Shoulder to the wall.

"Keep your hands under the water"

"Press down with your free hand to lift you up"

"Wide slow movements: Breaststroke type or Crawl type"

No floats.

Close to the wall.

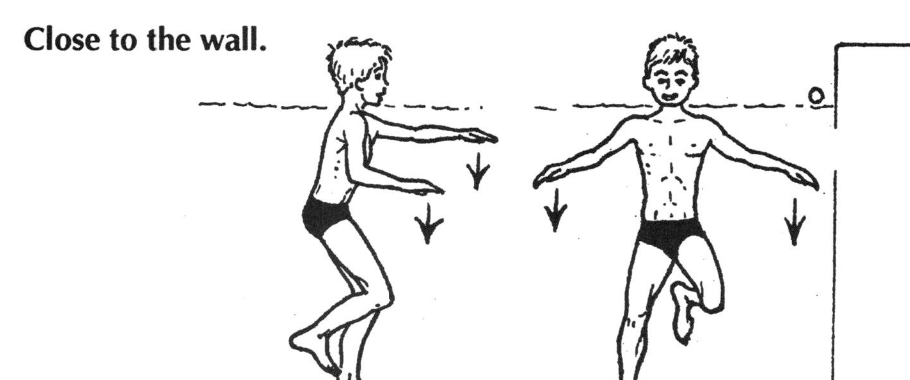

"Swim on the spot . The slower and wider, the easier"

"Press down with your hands"

PRACTICE | **TEACHING POINTS**

An easy way to submerge.

(More streamlined)

"Stand up straight with the object at the side of your foot. Your hand should be pointing straight down on top of it"

"Head up-jump up"

"Jump up high. Sink and squat on the bottom. Your hand should go straight on top of the object"

"Eyes open...blow out as you sink"

Mushroom float

"Hold your breath"
"Gently curl up into a tight ball"

"Can you touch your knees with your nose?"

An easy way to rotate.

1. Get a partner. "Ones & Twos". No.2 stands with legs wide apart.
2. No.1 stands behind No.2 with hands on partner's shoulders. This keeps the action close.

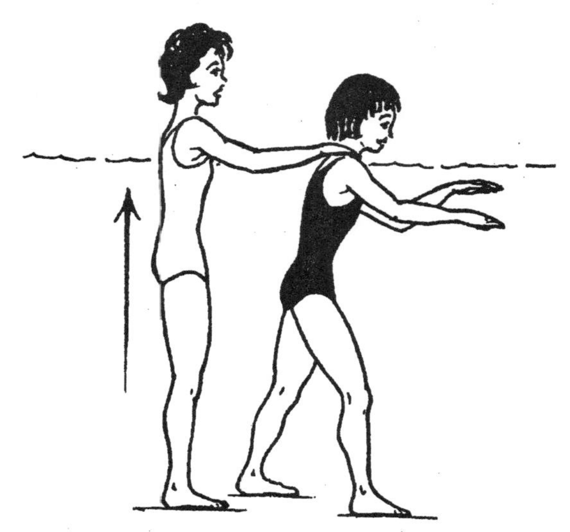

3. No.1 presses down on shoulders and **at the same time** jumps up high.
4. "Jump up...sink to the floor...roll forwards... ...now swim through partner's legs."

Shallow Water Method

Deep Water Method

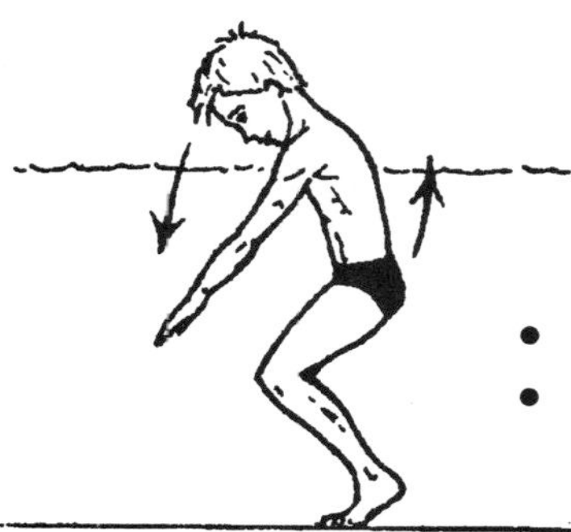

Both methods

- At least shoulder depth
- Start with the feet together

Rotation

Half a handstand
Hold this position for several seconds

"Roll your bottom upwards until out of the water"
"Imagine you are a duck looking for food"

Hands firmly on floor

Hands still holding rail

"Roll your hips out of the water **slowly**"

Streamlining

"When stable, stretch your legs up to the ceiling"

"Keep all your movements on the spot"
(i.e. no reaching forward)

Assuming the pre-requisites have been well taught and the skills achieved to a reasonable degree, moving pupils up on to the poolside for a shallow entry dive should not be difficult. Most problems arise when the shallow water work has been neglected, in particular the handstand - especially the 'half handstand' position at the rail, in deep water.

Check: The water is clear of other pupils.

The water is at least 1.8m or the full reach depth of the pupils, whichever is the greater.

The pupils are well organised.

They know to swim away from the point of entry.

Check: For rotation, (previously taught for the handstand).

Roll your bottom up – head down

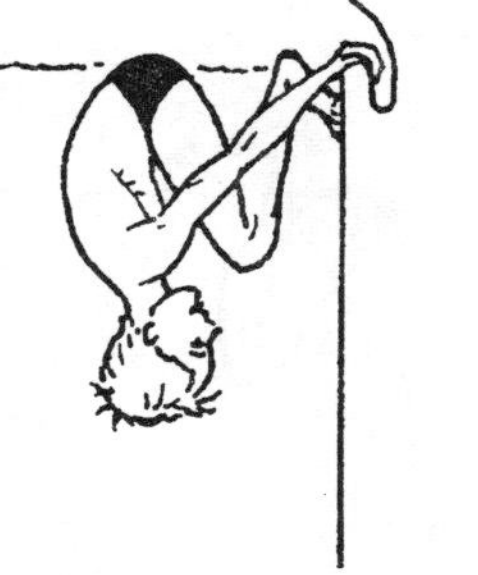

Check: The hands are linked together, mainly to protect the head, but also for streamlining.

Check: The entry position with a push and a glide.

Hands and feet together.

"Stretch from head to toe"

Can they hold the glide for a count of 6?

Finally combine all the above skills with a sitting dive, or better still a kneeling dive
Remember – First you roll, then you push

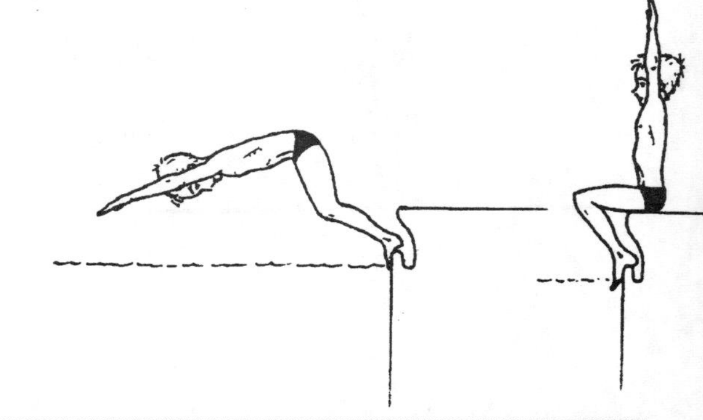

SHALLOW DIVING

The water should be at least 1.8m deep, or the full reach depth of the pupil, whichever is the greater.

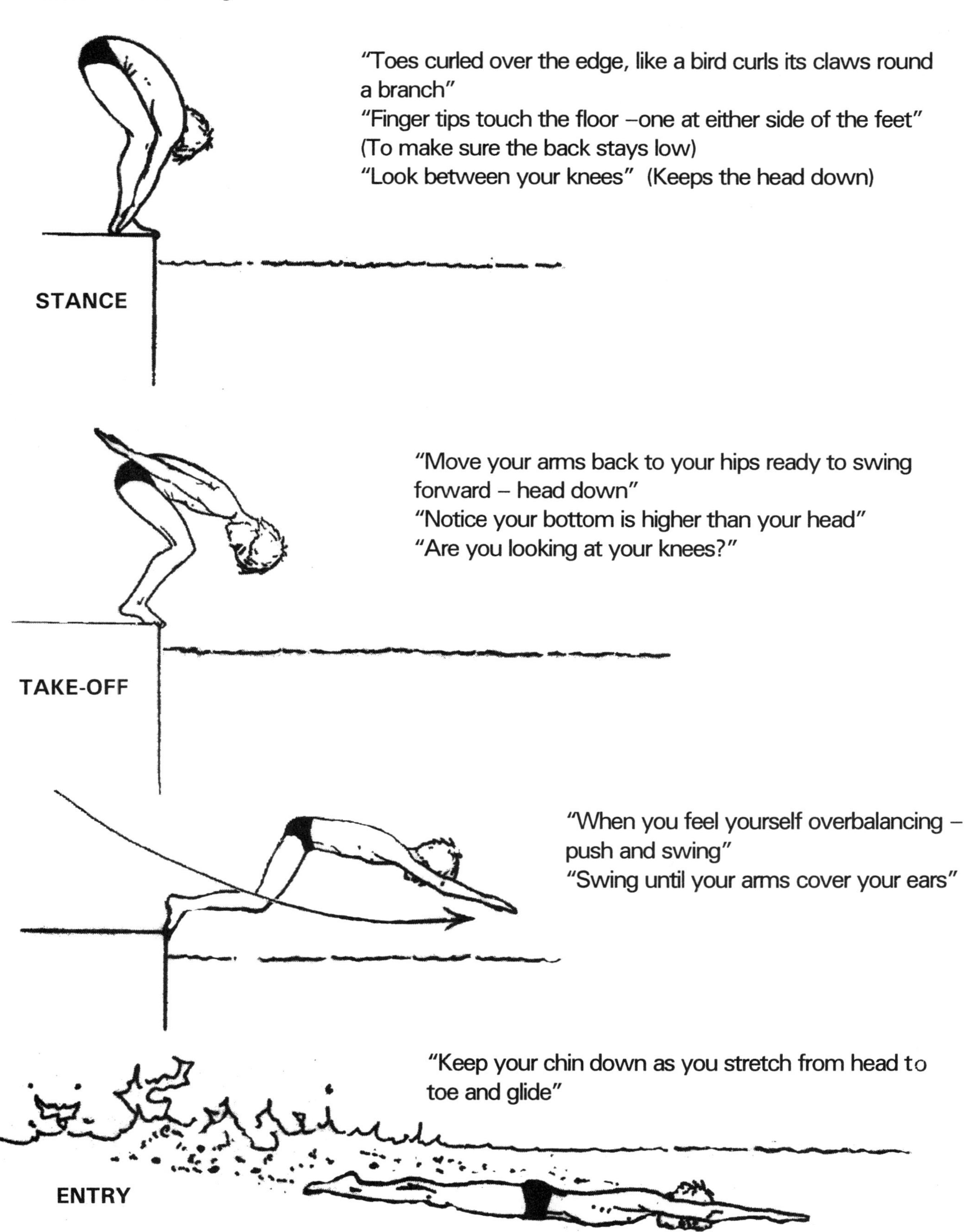

PRACTICE	TEACHING POINTS
Treading water. **Body vertical, and lift.**	"How high can you lift your shoulders out of the water?" "Kick down"
Kick down. **Body reaches up.**	"A vigorous kick down **at the same time** as your arms swing up above your head" "How high can you lift your chest out of the water?"
Streamlined. **Body now sinks.**	"Stretched from head to toe - sink"
	"As your feet near the bottom, rotate forwards and swim along the bottom"

EASY HEAD - FIRST SURFACE DIVE

PRACTICE | **TEACHING POINTS**

Swimming into handstand

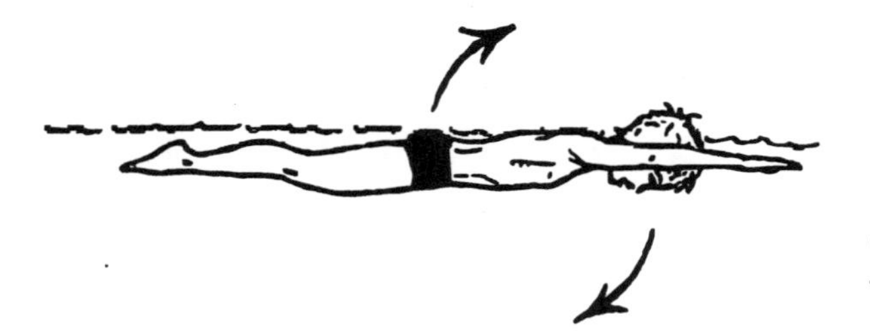

"Bottom up – head down"

"Vigorous pull back to the hips at the same time as bottom up to the ceiling"

Rotation – as in 'Handstands'

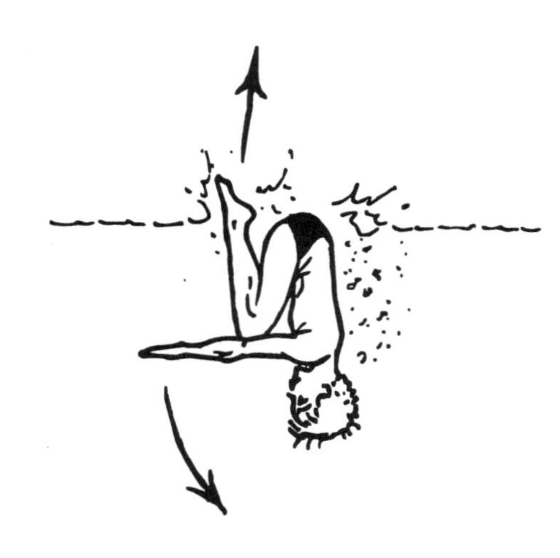

"Push down from the hips to lift your bottom up"

"When upside down (half a handstand) stretch to the bottom like an arrow"

Streamlined. Now sink

"Stretch with your legs glued together and still"

"Arms squashing ears"

"Hands held together"

N.B. Rotation can be developed by teaching a straight leg lift i.e. piked position

PRACTICE	TEACHING POINTS
Hand action.	Thumbs slightly tilted **upwards** as the arms move towards each other and **down** as they move away from each other

Standing in shallow water

Or on the side.

"Arms straight - swing from the shoulder"

"Hands under water - fingers together"

"Thumbs up - thumbs down"

"Sweep out then sweep in"

Toes under the rail.

Feel the action with the correct body position.

"Hips up and stretch"

"Hands working underneath your hips - to stop the legs sinking"

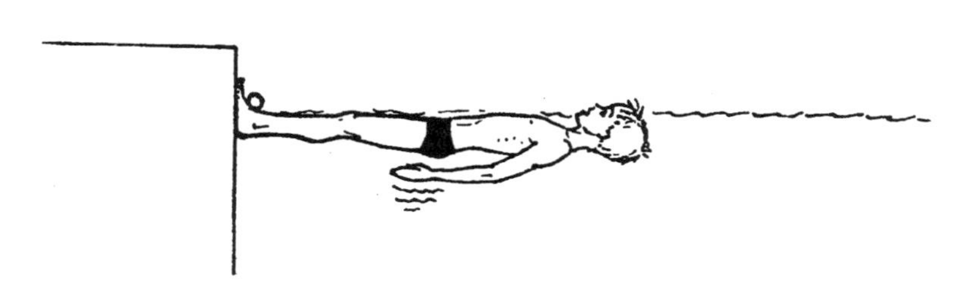

One float between the legs.

Feel the action in motion.

"Stretch your body"

"Continuous movement of your hands - **under** the hips"

Sculling head first.

"Stretch - keeping your legs together"

"Finger tips slightly up"

"Can you feel your toes at the surface?"

Head first: fingertips up. Feet first: finger tips down. Stationary: palms flat.

This section is different from the rest of the book, in that it is written as a narrative 'script' which you can use or adapt for your lessons.

It is intended to help you prepare for the ASA Personal Survival Awards, Levels One and Two. If you intend testing your pupils for these awards, you will need the ASA Awards Handbook, available from ASA Merchandising (address at rear of book). A useful book 'Survival in Cold Water' is also available from ASA Merchandising.

PERSONAL SURVIVAL

First Lesson.........

Setting The Scene: Explain that for the next four weeks they should imagine that the pool is the sea or a lake, and the water is so cold they would quickly get a headache if they swam in it.

"Imagine you are on a boat trip, and one of the passengers is an Olympic swimmer. The boat hits a submerged log, turns over, and everyone is thrown into the water."

"It may seem strange, but the Olympic swimmer would probably not survive much longer than an average swimmer like yourself. Why? The COLD WATER!"

The "Core" temperature.

"Think of the winter, when people can't start their cars because the engines are too cold. Well, we have an engine too, made up of our heart, lungs and liver, and it will stop too if it gets too cold.

The freezing water takes away the heat from our skin, and our engine gets colder and colder until it stops. The Olympic swimmer has just the same engine as you, and his will stop too!

It is very important to keep your head out of this very cold water. Why? Place your finger on top of your head and press hard. There's no fat there. It doesn't matter how fat or thin we are, there's no fat on top to keep our heads warm. And most of the heat from our engine escapes from the top of our head. In the olden days before central heating and double glazing, people's bedrooms were very cold, so they wore night caps on their heads!

See if you can keep your head dry throughout the lesson."

Action

"Imagine the side of the pool is a boat.

Find a way of getting into the water, and then swimming four widths, without getting your head wet.

How would you get in if the boat side was some distance above the water level?"

Ensure the water is at least full reach depth, then teach the straddle entry. Allow them to experiment with this, as well as sitting and swivelling in.

"Choose the entry you're best at, then tread water for two minutes. While you're there, try waving. Do you think you could keep waving for the whole two minutes?"

The selected entry and the ability to wave determine whether Level One or Level Two is appropriate.

"Also, can you think of three reasons why you should stay close to the scene of the accident?"

a. The rescue boat will find you more easily.

b. You'll find more things to support you near to the boat, like wood and plastic containers.

c. You'll save energy and body heat by not swimming.

Second Lesson.........

- Recap on heat loss, and the way their "engine" stops in the cold.
- Recap on methods of entry.
- Group your pupils into "swivellers" (Level One) and "straddlers" (Level Two)
- Tread water for two minutes, with Level Two waving for help.
- From treading water, swim 25m. Climb out.

Teaching the H.E.L.P. (Heat Escape Lessening Position):

Each pupil will need a piece of "debris" Eg a thick float or a large empty plastic squash bottle.

Get them into the water close to you, hugging their debris, squeezing their legs together and trying to keep still!

"Show me what would you do with your shoulders if you were waiting for a bus on a very cold day?" (Scrunch up to cover the NECK)

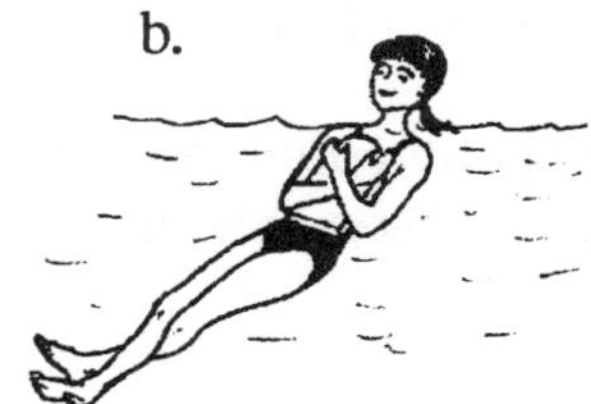

"Now show me what would you do with your arms on a cold day" (Squeeze in to cover ARMPITS, with elbows into cover RIBS).

"Now imagine you have gone to bed on a freezing night and you have forgotten to turn on your electric blanket! Show me what you do with your legs." (They curl up to cover the GROIN and the BACK of the KNEES, squeezing their legs together, - position (a) - and after a while may relax to position (b)).

- A board or flip chart will help.

Explain the meaning of **H**eat **E**scape **L**essening **P**osition

- Now tell them if they keep still in H.E.L.P. and hug their debris or life jacket they could survive up to 4 hours. If they fidget and lose heat this could be cut to 2 hours. If they swim off they will be lucky to last half an hour, and usually less than that.

NB These times are intended to be only an indication, and to make a point to the pupils (which they usually do).

Bring clothes next lesson!

Third Lesson: Dress Rehearsal.......

Recap on H.E.L.P. Check
they have brought the right clothing.

It is essential that all pupils swim along the side of the pool, within reach of a pole, when first swimming in clothes. Accidents happen when swimming strokes are restricted by clothing!

They swim a width in clothes. "Is it easier or more difficult?" ... **"More difficult!"**

They swim a second width. "Do you feel warmer or colder?" ... **"Warmer!"**

Group them together and discuss. "If it's more difficult to swim, but you feel warmer, why should you keep your clothes on?" ... "To keep your engine warm".

"How many of you have worn a wet suit? Are you wet or dry? You are actually wet, but you are warm so you feel dry. The water seeps in and your blood warms it up. Clothes do the same sort of thing."
"What clothes might you take off if you have time? ... Anything you feel is pulling you down, like heavy shoes, jackets etc"

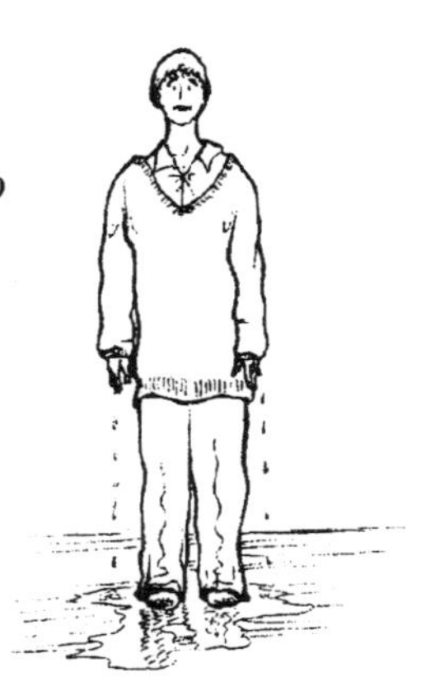

Teaching the huddle.

"You've kept your heat in so your engine is still warm! You can keep warmer still if you huddle together with your friends.

Imagine you are in an overcrowded bus or train. These are always very hot because people make a lot of heat. So if you huddle together in a group you can keep warm and keep one another cheerful!"

"Imagine the rescue boat has arrived. Do you throw your piece of debris away, or take it to the boat with you? ... Keep it with you!

The boat may take quite a long time to pick everyone up, or it may be full so you will have to wait for another!"

Waiting to get into the rescue boat.

Have them kick their way to the rescue boat (usually the teacher) hugging their debris, but without reaching for the side when they get there. Resume the H.E.L.P.

"Should you all climb onto the boat at the same time? ... No, it might capsize. So climb out five at a time."

"Is there a rail on the side of a boat? ... No! So climb out without using the rail." (Useful to imagine the rail is electrified!)

REMEMBER! Assessment next week. Bring your clothes!

Fourth Lesson: Final Assessment.........

Organization. You will need to be well organized to assess your pupils against the schedule of tests specified in the Awards Handbook.

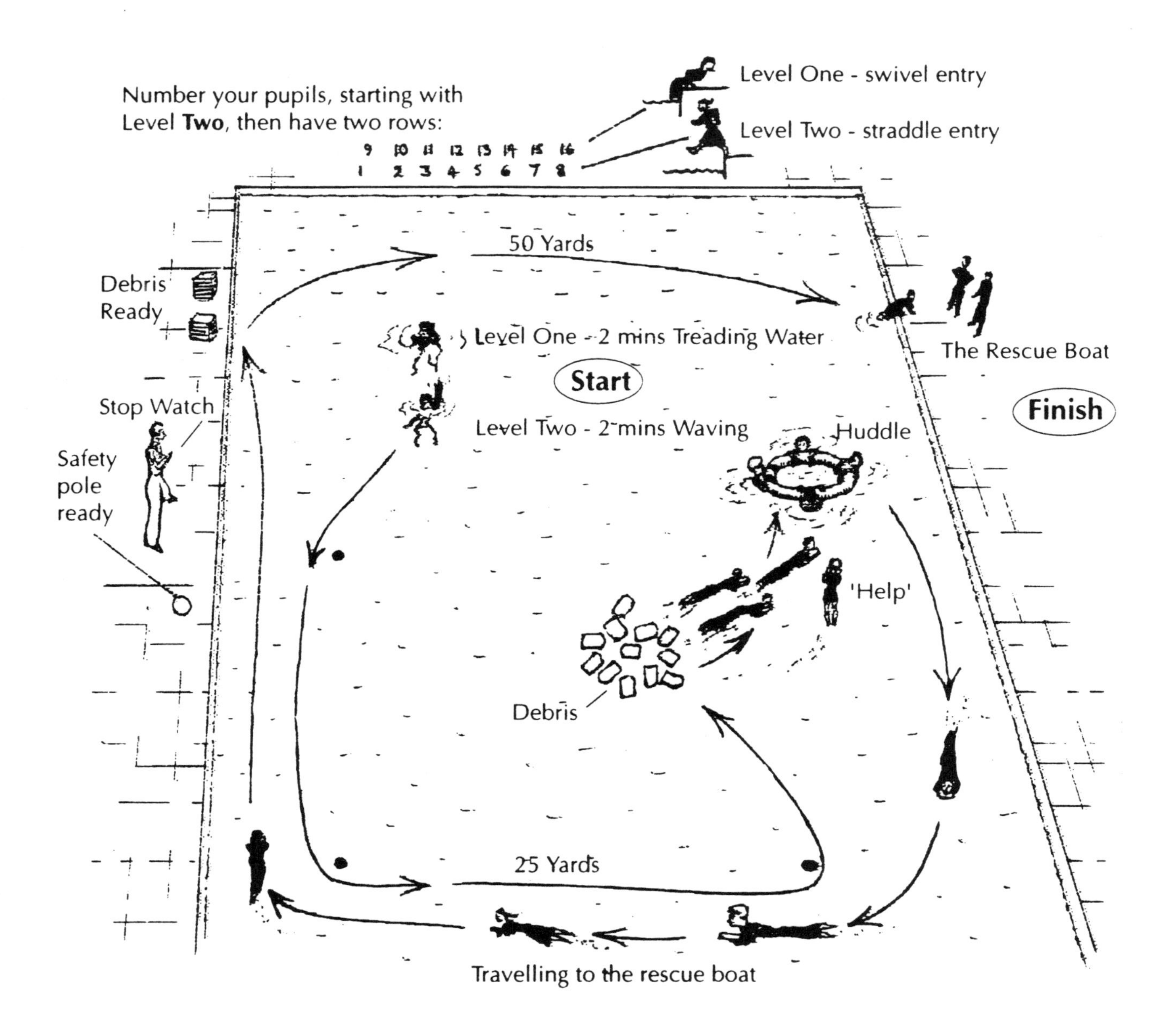

- Check the correct clothing.
- Start the assessment by sending them off in waves - Level Two first then Level One.
- Keep the weaker pupils nearer to the side, and have a safety pole to hand at all times - even the strongest can get into difficulty.
- Make sure they see the assessment as a learning process -they don't fail; they just drown!
- Have the "drowners" finish the test in their swimming costumes.

Questionning

Both ASA Awards require that pupils "answer three questions on when the skills learned might be used". This is a very important part of the assessment. If they haven't understood the principles the award will only be a badge.

- Bring all pupils together, not just the "survivors".
- Direct questions to the whole group, but take answers only from the survivors.
- Typical questions might be:

  "When you started the test you sat down and swivelled in, or straddled in. Why?"

  "The next thing you did was to tread water. Can you give me three reasons why you did this instead of swimming off?"

  "In the distance you saw some floating debris. What position did you take up when you reached it?"

  "What does each letter of H.E.L.P. mean?"

  "Why do you get into this position?"

  "Which parts of the body lose most heat?"

  "How long might you survive if you stay in this position?"

  "If there were several other people with you, what other position could you take up and why?"

  "Swimming with clothes is difficult. Why should you keep them on?"

  "How do wet clothes keep you warm?"

  "What might you take off if you had time?"

  "The rescue boat has arrived, but it is some way away from you. Do you take your debris with you? Why?"

  "Whilst travelling to the boat why should you hug your debris?"

  "Having reached the boat, there are several people waiting to get in. Why should you stay in the H.E.L.P.?"

  "Why is it important to get out without touching the rail or steps?"

- Ask for "Hands Up" - no shouting out!
- Congratulate a good answer publicly.
- Congratulate those that are clearly "with-it" and ensure the results are recorded. It is suggested that these pupils, and the "drowners" are now sent to get changed.
- Probe the rest further for understanding; they may merely be shy. (Don't forget to record their results too.)
- A "No Understanding - No Award this time" philosophy is suggested, at the same time encouraging those who haven't made it to try again.

Mathematics

1. Money - Entrance fees
   - Cost of coach/train journey to the pool
2. Measurement - Length, width, depth (estimation)
   - Volume of cuboids, displacement
   - How many lengths of the pool do you have to swim to cover certain distances?
   - Distances in imperial and metric measures, conversion graphs
   - Measuring times
3. Data Handling - Collecting and collating speeds and distances
   - Calculating mean speeds
   - Representing data collected on graphs
   - Inserting data collected into a database
4. Angles - Full, half and whole turns
   - Turning through a number of degrees

History

1. Romans - Bath
2. Victorians - Seaside bathing
3. Famous swimmers - Olympics

Science

1. Measuring the temperature of the water
2. Measuring body temperature before and after exercise
3. Measuring pulse rates before and after exercise
4. How does sound travel underwater?
5. What can you hear underwater?
6. Floating, sinking and surface tension
7. Resistance vs streamlining
8. Body structure and muscles
9. Pollution - clean beaches
10. Keeping the pool clean - chlorine

English

1. Listening to instructions
2. Devise a list of rules for the swimming pool
3. Creative Writing
   - Poems about the sport, sounds at the swimming pool etc.
   - Write a story about a long distance swim. Include thoughts and feelings
4. Related reading
   - 'Night Swimmers': Betsy Byers
   - 'Water Babies': Kingsley
   - 'Little Mermaid': Fairy tale
   - 'Poseidon': Mythology

Geography

1. Locate the swimming pool on a map
2. Draw a map to show the route taken by the coach to the swimming pool
3. Draw the swimming pool to scale
4. Instructions given in the pool relating to compass directions
5. Seaside resorts at home and abroad

Languages

1. Giving instructions in a foreign language
2. Games

Design Technology

1. Make a scale model of the swimming pool
2. Design a leisure complex to include swimming pool, slides, changing rooms etc.
3. What is the best shape for a swimming pool to hold the maximum volume of water?
4. Design a boat to carry a load a certain distance and test it in the pool
5. Arrange a swimming gala for six schools, design posters and organise events

By Staff at Grimsdyke Middle School, Harrow.

Further Reading

	Published by
Cregeen and Noble: Swimming Games and Activities	AC Black
Introduction to Swimming Teaching and Coaching	ASA
Swimming Teaching and Coaching: Level 1	ASA
Survival in Cold Water	ASA
Awards Handbook	ASA

Addresses (at the time of writing)

- (For awards and books) ASA Merchandising, 1 Kingfisher Enterprise Park, 50 Arthur St, Redditch, Worcestershire B98 8LG Tel: 01527 514 288 Fax 01527 514 277
- (For education and other enquiries) ASA Education Department, Harold Fern House, 18 Derby Square, Harold Fern House, Derby Square, Loughborough, Leics LE11 0AL Tel: 01509 618 721 Fax 01509 618 701

To order more copies of this book, or its companion volumes, please send a cheque with the slip below. You get a discount if your total order is for 10 books or more. Prices include postage and packing.

Total no. of books

1 - 9 .... £6.50 each
10 - 29 .... £5.50 each
30 - 99 .... £5.00 each

Send to: Anne Eakin, 48 Carpenters Wood Drive, Chorleywood, Herts. WD3 5RJ.
Tel: 01923 284 522 E-mail: rs-a_eakin@tiscali.co.uk

...✂...

Name and address for delivery: --

(Please write clearly) --

		No. required
The Non-Swimmer	*getting them started*	
Swimming	*teaching early practices*	
The Competent Swimmer	*teaching more advanced practices*	
	Total books	
	Amount enclosed	£

Cheques payable to A. Eakin, please. Thank you for your order